MW00465392

The Journey of a
Transforming Soul

Josie Thomas

BookLeaf
Publishing

The Journey of a Transforming Soul © 2022
Josie Thomas

All rights reserved.

Presentation by *BookLeaf Publishing*

Web: www.bookleafpub.com

E-mail: info@bookleafpub.com

ISBN:

First edition 2022

DEDICATION

To my Bestie for showing me this new path and
encouraging me to step outside my comfort
place with all the loves, thank you so much.

To myself for being brave enough to share this
experience of my life, and opening new doors,
thank you.

To you the Soul reading this for what ever made
you pick my book up, may it bring you peace
and hopefully a better look on yourself and life.
Thank you so much!!!

Time

Tick tock the clock strikes 6
Another hour gone
Another hour to pass
Yet every hour feels the same

A tricky mess time can be
Moving slow at times it should be fast
To fast when there's no rush
Yet on and on it goes

Can't waste time
Because you don't have any
Yet there's nothing to do
When you have minutes to spare

A playful trickster time can be
Fooling around like nothing's wrong
But everything is backwards
And the hands keep marching on

Seconds turn to minutes
Which turn to hours, days
Then weeks, then months and
Eventually years

How you choose to spend your time

Is up to you alone
Spend it wisely
You never know when your time is up

Looking In Mirrors

There's a mirror in my bedroom
I look in it everyday
To see the same reflection
Of who I'm supposed to be
Brown hair
Brown eyes
A nose
Two lips
And I wonder if the girl I see
Is who I really am
So full of sunshine on rainy days
A ball of fun when laughter is gone
If so then why do I feel blue
Like I'm falling in a hole
A hole with no begining or end
Just darkness all-around
This is the wrong reflection
The person I see is not really me
With her round shiney eyes
With her stunning bright smile
She's just my imagination
Of who I pretend to be
What will the mirror show
If it revealed the real me
Dark hollow eyes lacking emotion

Will I have the strength to see

Screaming Whispers

It feels like all I want to do is cry
The pain inside's too much
Each day my luck runs dry
Nothing I do goes my way
Everyone says I'm a failure
So I guess that's all I am
There's nothing left for me
Let me die tonight
The light I see gets dimmer
The whispers say it'll be okay
Voices tell me no one will miss me
That I have nothing to live for
They say go ahead grab the blade
Slide it cross my wrist
I hear the voices everyday
How much louder they've become
I'll listen to them this one time
The blade sparkles in my hand
Wrist bare and soft
I'm ready to forget the pain inside my heart

Behind My Bedroom Door

I'll put on a smile
When I want to cry
I'll make you think I'm okay
Even though I want to die
Things are fine for now
At least to you they are
But behind my bedroom door
That's when all the tears fall

Learn and Remember

You give your heart away
To a person you love dear
Yet in return
You get it back
Shattered into pieces
Torn to shreds
Burnt to ash
Then all you can do
Is try and be strong
For the next time you fall in love
You'll learn and remember
What you get
When you give your heart away

F.M.L.

It's over and it's done
I'm through with living
Pretending everything's fine
I need the pain to end
All the darkness
Anger and hatred
All can be forgotten
Just a knife to my chest
A gun to my head
Now's the time to say goodbye
I'm sorry and I loved you
Find all the ones that hurt me
Tell them thanks your job is done
I'll do it with a few regrets
Lies I left unsaid
Hopefully my secrets
Will be revealed
When I'm hanging from a thread

Cutting Tears

The pains to much I cannot hold it in
I need to find a way to let it go
Without letting you see my troubles
So with silent fingers I'll grab that blade
And secretly release the blood filled tears
One stroke and the love is gone two strokes and
so is the anger
Three, then four, five and six
One by one the feelings disappear
And by the tenth my heart is numb
And my leg is two
But there's nothing more to feel
Everything washed away with the river of blood
that flows down my leg
For now everything is fine, no pain or sorrow
Just a cut up empty body
And it's alright with me even when
The cuts scar up and the emotions come
flooding back
It'll be fine cause I'll grab that blade
The one that freed me from myself
The one that let me cry out my feelings
Without shedding a tear in my eye
So now you'll never know I'm crying through a
blade.

Ask Me

You ask me why I cut
Why I always cry
You ask me why it is exactly that I wish to die
If you can look inside my eyes, my heart, mind
and soul
The answers right in front of you
But if you're to blind to see
Then I'll only say this once
There won't be another chance
When I cry my eyes swell up and this is the
reason why
I see the hate and anger filling up each room
How I long to escape before I'm totally
consumed
But I always leave to late
I see the pain of memories lies and games that
block my future
I cut because of thoughts that stack up in my
head
Each broken dream and wish that never came
true
Slips away with every track left from the blade
I cut because it's my pain relief from
The blackness that grows inside

Which is the reason I want to die
I'm slowly slipping away
This darkness is taking over a little more each
day
I lost myself who I was and who I could become
All lost in the shadow corners of my nightmares,
fears and heart
Parts of me I can't get back no matter what I do
I've grown up so young with all the stress I
never should have known
My life already passing me by
You now know why I cut and cry and why I
want to die
I won't stand here and listen to why you say you
care
No more questions no more answers it's time to
say goodbye

Swimming In A Liquor Bottle

Staring down the glass neck
Envisioning the bottom
Standing at the bottle's lips
Diving right on in
Splashing in the sweet spice of rum
Riding the waves of summer wine
Started just to have some fun
Kept it up to keep the pain at bay
Till all you want is to do
Is swim in that liquor bottle
Then the tides start rolling in
As tequila hurricanes begin merging
With whirlpools of Four Loko
Leaving you half drowned
Washed up on the bathroom floor

Forgiveness is Divine

Each journey comes to a point
When the traveler finds
Their footsteps heavy
Muddied up with past regrets
From causing pain to loved ones
Innocents who never deserved
That kind of treatment done
Weighed down by self loathing
Caused by consequences
Of misjudged choices
Each action that caused harm
Mentally physically emotionally
As travelers on life's journey
We cross many streams
We can choose to jump across
Keeping on our way
Or soak and wash the guilt away
I choose to heal in the streams of forgiveness
Taking a faithful dive on in
Forgiving the times I let myself be hurt
By not just others but myself included
I'm forgiving those who kicked me while I was
down
"'Wise men say forgiveness is divine'"
And with these divine forgiving waters

I wash away the muddy regret
The self loathing caked on in layers
I forgive so I can continue my travels
Without the weight of the past

I'll Be Strong For You

When you cry
I'll let my shirt soak up your tears
And when you're done
I'll wipe the rest away

When you feel alone
I'll be there with a hug
Wrap my arms around you
Never let you go

I'll hold you up
If your knees get weak
I'll be your shinning star
When darkness blinds your way

Go ahead and cry
It's okay to be afraid
Cause I'll be your strength
When yours has flown away

Goodbye From the Heart

You left this world behind
Left family and friends
Between us things fell apart
But I'll forever love you will all my heart

In the next life you'll find peace
And we'll even meet again
I forgive you of the pain
Please forgive me of the same

This spot in my heart is forever yours
Thank you for all you taught me
Thank you for the love and time spent
For the memories we shared

All the things I lost time to say
Yet I know my feelings will reach your heart
No matter where your soul ventured to
My love will reach your consciousness

An Enemy's Love

Always gotta love thy enemies
Cause all they doing is showing love
Keeping the spot light on you
And you on their mind
However in the spotlight
How you act shows your character's truth
Are you giving the same love
Your enemies are giving you
Or do you respond with
The kind of love that's deeply pure
I choose to love them purely
For they need that love to heal
The parts of them they see in me
That make em choose to be my enemy

Life's Music

Tune into the beat of life
Listen with ears of love
Then you'll start to hear
Voices of each soul sing

From the pacing pigeons pitter-patters
As he makes his home complete
To skateboards clashing with concrete
As high-fives and cheers get passed around

Sounds created by inspired souls
Each harmonized in one melody
Following with the soul's rhythm
Enjoy the songs of life

Tune yourself into the Universe
Listen with all your heart
Let free the beat inside
Play yourself to the music of Life

Hopeful Star

Do you think there can be more
Then what your teary eyes lead you to believe
Through the smoke of fear
Answers become unclear and still you try to see

After so long the faithful path
You've walked on so many years
Grows weeds of lies and broken dreams
Causing you to trip in words of poisoned thorns

Shadows from your haunted past
Creep slowly forming tangled spider webs
To hold you from what your future holds

All this chaos manipulates your heart
Clouding possible escape
Twinkling in the distance of your grasp
Wrap your fingers tight around this star of hope

The tighter you squeeze the flames ignite
Shadows run from rays of love
The weeds the thorns all vanish
Leaving your path visible once more

Secrets From the Stars

I'm going to tell you a little secret
One I've held on to very dear
At night each little twinkling star
Comes knocking at my window
To whisper words of truth; of love
And of darkness and despair
I have a little secret
It's been weighing on my mind
About the dancing trees
And the wind who dances in time
 The trees never moving
From the moment their lives start
The wind she's always changing
Dancing from tree to tree
Always on the go
They form the perfect dance of jealousy
The trees would love to move, to flow
The wind in turn would enjoy to have
A place to lay and have a night to rest
I have a little secret one that needs to be
revealed
Of the ocean oh so blue
Her only friend our lovely moon
They keep each other company

Way up late at night
Whispering what they each would do
If they could leave their precious home
The moon he wishes to swim in the ocean's
never ending waves
While glancing at her friend the ocean she longs
to fly
To sail high above the world
Who holds her firmly on the ground
The stars have told me one last secret
One last little truth
That even though each of our friends
Long for a life they'll never know
Day by day they live
Knowing they are happiest being home

Fear's False Deception

Fear guards the door to freedom
Keeping you from full expression
Just let it go and fly
Away from the suppression
Flow with the manifestation
This flow of perception
Disguised as a deception
Fooling the five senses
Setting us free internally
Finding True Reality

Holding on to Dreams

Dreams move life, give it a goal
Some may change, others forgotten
I'm fighting for mine right now
No retreating, No surrendering!
Transforming dreams to reality
Guided by the flow of love
Writing stories on beaches
Songs on mountain tops
Under the Northern Lights
Movies and plays will be constructed

Thanks for Finding Me

My dearest friend
I owe you so much
You found me in my darkest moment
To my bewilderment
You began to share your Light
Thank you for all you taught me
And what you still have to share
Thank you for pulling me out
Of that depression and despair
For helping me find my own Light
To embrace the Goddess within
Words are not enough to express
The gratitude I have
Thanks for finding me
I'm glad I found you to

Ask Me Again

You once asked me why I cut
Why I always cry
You asked once why exactly
That I wished to die
Ask me again
But this time ask why I want to live
When you look inside my heart
You'll find the answers deep within
I no longer see hatred filling up rooms
I'm now looking through eyes of love
Which is why I want to live
To share the beauty of life
With all those I hold dear
I want to help those other souls
Who like me once upon a time
Are wishing they would die
That the deepest love we all seek
Can only be found inside
And once you find that inner Love
You'll find your will to live

Being the Flame

As I look within my soul
I see my flame of life
Fueled with love
Watch it ignite
Glowing brighter then the moon
On even the darkest of nights
Feel the passion to live get stronger
Let it grow till I'm all consumed
Wearing my royal attire
Heat from my flames
Radiates the same love
Healing all those who touch it
I am the flames of life
The flames of light
Of Love